A Home for Flap the Cat

by Susi Jones
illustrated by Jaime Smith

Phonics Skill: Consonants Blends
High-Frequency Words: *one, two, three, four, five*

PEARSON
Scott
Foresman

Nat and Nan hop and skip.

One hop, Nan!

One skip, Nat!

Nat and Nan stop.

Nat and Nan stop for

Flap the Cat.

Two claps for Flap the Cat.
Clap, clap for Flap!

Can Flap the Cat sip three drops?

Flap the Cat can sip three drops.

Sip, sip, sip, Flap!

I spot four dots on Flap the Cat.

Dot, dot, dot, dot!

Do you spot dots on him?

I spot one, two, three, four, five!

Dot, dot, dot, dot, dot!

Five dots on Flap the Cat.

Flap the Cat likes to sit
on my lap!
Sit, Flap, sit!